FUNNY BONES

Rib-tickling comics from
Medical Economics

Edited by

James D. Hendricks

Executive Editor
Medical Economics Magazine

Medical Economics Books
Oradell, N.J. 07649

Cover Design: John Newcomb

Design: Brianne Carey Wright

All cartoons have appeared in
medical economics magazine

Library of Congress Cataloging-in-Publication Data

Hendricks, James D.
　Funny bones.

　1. Medical economics—Caricatures and cartoons.
2. American wit and humor, Pictorial.　I. Title.
NC1429.H395A4　1988　741.5'973　　88-1683
ISBN 0-87489-486-7

Medical Economics Company Inc.
Oradell, New Jersey 07649
Printed in the United States of America

"Are you guys sure you haven't seen the mice any-where?"

"Watch your step. She went on a diet today."

Sorry, right number

I asked a new patient who had referred her to us. "No one, " she said. She explained that her home phone number was just one digit different from our 24-hour number. "I'm always getting calls from patients trying to reach you" she continued, "and I decided so many people couldn't be wrong."

— *Lawrence R. Pankau,* MD

"She'd be about right for you. That was painted in 1874."

"Look, the clinic can't treat you until the government gets all its information. Now, what's your family crest?"

"First of all, you cannot file a return signed 'Anony-mous'."

Easy come, easy go

For years, Old Joe bumbled into my office after drawing his pay from a succession of odd jobs and then disappearing on a binge. Invariably, he'd promise to take care of my fee Tuesday. That day never came, but I put up with him out of sympathy and because of his irresistible self-confidence. The last time I saw him, he varied his pay-Tuesday routing. He grinned, the added: "Doc, you're such a good sport, put down two more bucks for yourself."

— *Donald C. Haugh,* MD

"You'll like it here. They treat you like a person rather than a number."

"George, your hiccups are gone!"

"Just wait 'til the next time Harold calls me a hypochon-
driac."

Scared away

As I discussed a patient's case in my consultation room. I wasn't aware that the 4-year-old grandson she'd brought along was looking around wide-eyed. I later learned that he'd paid particular notice to the 18-inch, built-to-scale skeleton that reposes on my desk. When they left the office, the boy told his grandmother that he'd never want to go to *that* doctor. When she asked why, he said: "Didn't you see what he does to little kids?" — *Howard J. Ickes,* MD

"Of course, you still have to have sunshine."

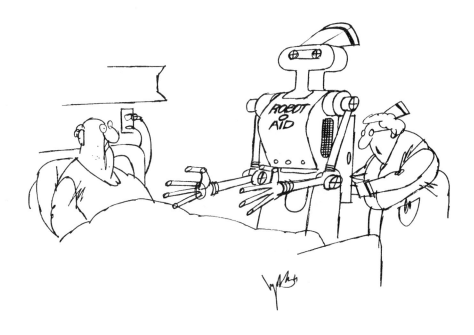

"I've programmed it for your enema."

Enough is enough

The elderly woman who was draped for sigmoidoscopy seemed confused and not at all cooperative. An intern held her in the knee-chest position as a resident commenced the procedure. After much wiggling and yelping and moaning, the patient suddenly became very quiet. Then a small voice came from under the sheet: "Boys, if you stop right now, I promise I won't tell a soul."

— Bennett E. Uhlig, MD

"Remember, walk like Charlie Chaplin. They get a big kick out of it."

"Okay, I hit it, and it went into the little hole. Now, let's go home."

"I know exactly what you're going to say."

Truth and consequences

One recent Friday morning, I got a call from a rather agitated patient. He'd injured his ankle a week before, and I'd sent him to a hospital emergency department for X-rays that apparently showed he'd sustained only a bad sprain. Now the ED had phoned him, saying that a review of the films indicated a possible fracture and advising him to return for further studies. "You ought to get right back over there." I told him. "Hell, no!" he replied. "I'm not going back there until Monday. *They* made the mistake. Now let them suffer."

— *Donald R. Stoltz,* MD

"Thank you for bringing this to my attention, Scroggs.
I'll speak to our nutritionist."

"Don't bite it. I have to check Daddy next."

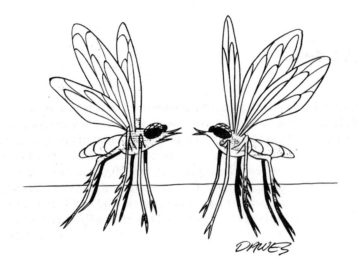

"For pity's sake, Hortense—We're fruit flies. We don't have time for a long, meaningful relationship."

Special delivery

Screams were heard one night from the alley two floors below the ward where I was on duty as an intern. The security guards who went to investigate reported that a woman was about to have a baby in a car. An attending physician rushed down with me to deliver the infant in the car's front seat. Later, I asked the second woman, who'd been driving the car, how they happened to end up in our blind alley. "My daughter was due at Boulevard General Hospital," she explained, "but on the way her labor pains got so bad that I knew we'd never make it in time. Then I saw the sign saying 'Sinai Hospital Delivery Entrance'— and I just pulled in."

— *Ronald Zack,* MD

"Relax, Mr. Tuttle. Who ever heard of lightning striking a bedpan?"

"It's the babysitter. She wants to know where we keep the homeowners policy."

"That's what I hate about Astroturf!"

Social visit

When the mother of a 7-year-old boy I'd treated for an ear infection brought him back to my office, she told me the family had just returned from a trip to Disneyland. It was a slow day, so I took a few minutes to put him at his ease by comparing notes with him on "Small World" and some of the other attractions. It was then quick work to examine him and find everything normal. "Mom," I heard him whisper as they were leaving, "the doctor spent most of the time talking about Mickey Mouse. Are you going to have to pay him?"   — *Willis M. Fong,* MD

"I'll start the fire while you read him his rights."

"Nobody bought me a damned thing!"

First things first

Insisting that her little boy be seen immediately, the young mother tearfully told me that he'd fallen out of a shopping cart at the supermarket and hit his head on a concrete floor. I asked how long ago it had happened. "Couldn't have been more than half an hour," she said. "Right after I got home and put the meat in the refrigerator, I rushed over here." — *Lyman R. Feinauer,* MD

"Feldknapp! You know very well that's not authorized procedure!"

"I'm sorry, Ralph, but it just dawned on me that I have a dog that growls, a parrot that swears, a stove that smokes, and a cat that stays out all night. Why in the world would I need a husband?"

Chilly source

The patient suddenly shuddered as I was palpating her abdomen. "Gosh," she said, "your fingers are awfully cold." I smiled and lightly replied, "Maybe that has something to do with the new diet I'm on." She let that sink in for a moment and then she asked: "What do you eat? Frozen foods?"

— *Oliver H. Nadeau,* MD

"I know what it *isn't*. But I wish I knew what it *is* that he's keeping score on."

"You call that justice? Only twelve people out of two hundred million said I was guilty!"

"Okay, buddy, let's hear your version."

"Ah, gee—now I'll *never* be teller-of-the-month."

"Merry Christmas morning, everybody! Did you remember to buy batteries for the kids' toys?"

Pride goeth

As the center of attention at a family gathering, I related my experiences during my first six months as a doctor. One relative asked how many patients I'd lost. "Only one," I replied, "and he was 95 years old." My wings were quickly clipped as 79-year-old Granddad wryly observed: "He was doing pretty good until you got hold of him."

— *Carolyn Gerald,* MD

"Why didn't he sue someone?"

"I'm sorry, but we don't have one for proctologists."

"As soon as we get home, you call the Better Business Bureau."

No rush

At a nursing home, I asked an elderly patient routine questions, such as why he was there, how old he was, and what medicines he was taking. Each time, his response was a mumbled "I don't know" or "I don't remember." My frustration must have become evident to him because he then gave me a reassuring grin and said: "Go on, ask me anything you want. I'll be here all day."

— *Richard Broadhead,* MD

"It's for my grandson. I don't know the artist's name, but the record sounds like natural childbirth."

"With all due respect to your horoscope, Mrs. Meriwether, I say we operate *today*."

"You never heard of this patient before in your life? Say...unless I think of something better, that's not a bad malpractice defense."

Neatness doesn't count

For pediatric allergy diagnosis, I've found it helpful to learn as much as I can about such home environment factors as exposure to certain kinds of furniture, pillows, and rugs. I began one history-taking by asking a 15-year-old patient what was on the floor in her bedroom. Without hesitation, she gave me a one-word answer. "Clothes," she said.   — *Gilbert L. Fuld,* MD

"Miss Jones, that was easily the most beautiful blood-curdling scream I've ever heard."

Thumb-in-mouth disease

As a young physician, I learned a lesson in thinking twice before you speak. A recovering patient asked if I'd like to take home one of the plants he'd received during his stay at the hospital. "Thanks, Sam," I said, "but I'd better not. I have such rotten luck that everything I touch seems to die." Small wonder that Sam refused to let me examine him on all the remaining days before he was discharged.
— *Matthew Frankel,* MD

"Good morning, sweetheart. Whew—what a breath!
What did you eat last night?"

"And what did the terrorists do after they forced you to drink the six-pack?"

"Well, if it's any satisfaction to you, we fired the guy who gave you the estimate."

Long abstinence

Going over the list of questions routinely put to patients on admission to our hospital's holding area, a nurse asked an elderly gentlemen: "Have you had anything since midnight?" Without batting an eye, he replied: "Not since 1948."

— *James F. Rambasek*, MD

"Try Reveille."

"What's the matter? Last night you couldn't get *enough* scotch."

"We're really rolling today. He's ready for his three o'clock appointment, and it's only four-thirty."

Double indemnity

Called by the fire department because a man had collapsed on the street, I found he had died. Just as I was reporting that to the head of the rescue unit, the medical examiner's car pulled up. "Great!" the fireman exclaimed. "You can't find a doctor when you're sick, but when you're dead you get two."

— *J. Clement Griffin,* MD

"He left six different wills with six different lawyers."

"I've never seen the zoo so crowded."

"And here's a get-well threat from your boss."

If the shoe fits

It had been several months since a patient had first been treated for genital warts. "It's about time," he said tartly when I told him the last remaining wart on his penis should disappear after his next treatment. I explained that wart removal can be a slow process. "Just the other day," I added, "a woman was here for her final visit exactly a year after she first came in with warts on her foot. She brought an anniversary cake shaped like a foot." "What shape cake," he snapped, "should I bring?"

— *Ralph G. Bennett,* MD

"Now, sir, is there any particular reason you wish to return the bottle of after-shave?"

"Well, there goes heaven."

"He's gone to a doctor. He smiled absentmindedly and got a terrible pain in the face."

Paternal pangs

One midnight, I was awakened by an anxious phone call from a man whose wife was about due for her first delivery. I advised him to keep timing her pains. After several more calls during the night, when it appeared that the patient was actually in labor, I said: "Well, now it's time to meet me at the hospital." His heavy breathing continued and then he asked: "Should I take my wife along?"
— *H. Melvin Radman*, MD

"I've seen the statistics, and I'm quitting!"

"You'll have to make that a dollar and a half, sir. I went on overtime at five o'clock."

"Hi, Gladys—back again?"

No problem

"The doctor can't fit you in until the day after tomorrow," said the temporary office helper we'd hired just that morning. She was talking to a woman who complained of having had back pains for several weeks. "I may be dead by then," the caller irately exclaimed. "Don't worry," she was reassured, "the doctor won't charge for the canceled appointment." — *William Klompus,* MD

"You're new here. I forgot to tell you to jump back when you unlock the door."

"Be careful, now. Teachers can sense fear."

"I think he'd look better on the other wall."

To tell the tooth

The elderly lady had been brought into the emergency room after falling on an icy pavement. The way she kept her lips so tightly clenched indicated she was in great pain. Thinking that even a brief jolt might hurt her more, I told her to grit her teeth before we lifted her onto the X-ray table. "Better wait till you send someone for them," she said as she unclasped her lips. "They're in my handbag."   — *H.P. Sawyer Jr.*, MD

"I paint what I see."

"He's always doing things to ridicule my cooking. Yesterday, he threw up."

"Some school! They won't let you pray *or* cuss!"

Trick or treatment?

One of the Halloween monsters who rang my doorbell was a youngster so grotesquely costumed as to be unrecognizable When I dropped a handful of candy bars into his bag, already bursting with goodies, he grinned behind his mask. "See what you get," he said, "when you make house calls."

— *Benjamin K. Silverman,* MD

"Well, I guess I'd better hang up now."

"See here, Foster, this is *heaven*. You don't have to *suffer* to stay healthy."

"We'd better get out of here before they think we did it!"

Playing the odds

One of my patients, a hard-working undertaker, insisted on being discharged from the hospital sooner than I thought advisable. After vainly trying to reason with him, I said: "By the way, I'm curious. How did you happen to pick me as your physician?" He never changed his deadpan expression as he replied: "Nothing to it. I checked the records and found you wrote the fewest death certificates."   — *Philip R. Alper,* MD

"Which party doesn't concern me. I just vote for the underdog."

"We don't have any requests, but maybe you should play
'Taps' for our waiter."

Checkout counter

"Look, Toby," my patient's husband said to his 4-year-old son at the window of our hospital's nursery. "That's your new little sister." Wide-eyed, Toby noticed the infant's wristband. "Golly," he exclaimed, "she still has her price tag on!"

— *Herbert L. Ruben,* MD

"And then one day, I forgot my access code, my security password, my bank card code, my Social Security number, and my nine-digit Zip Code."

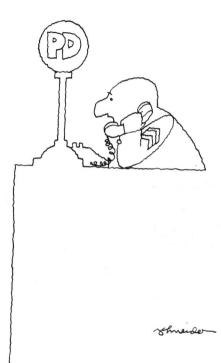

"We're a little understaffed tonight. Do you have anything handy you could hit the burglar with?"

Don't look now

One Sunday after surgery following injury to my spleen in a car accident, I found myself next to a woman friend in church. She asked me how I was. Slipping my hand under my suit jacket, I replied: "I must be healing because it itches. Look the other way if I scratch." She smiled and said, "The same to you, I'm just getting over a hysterectomy." — *M. Neil Rogers,* MD

"And this is Mrs. Whitaker. She teaches sex education."

"Well, we sure bungled that honeymoon."

"Mr. Fensterwald is next. He's having a problem with flatulence."

Early warning

The screaming 3-year-old had to be restrained by two nurses and an orderly. My colleague, who was trying to examine the child's eyebrow laceration, noticed the incipient swelling and discoloration. He told his mother: "Billy will be lucky if he gets through this with nothing more than a black eye." The mother shrugged. "Don't worry about it, Doctor," she said. "He's a holy terror at home too."

— *Mark Thoman*, MD

"Remember the good old days when a guy didn't have to watch his wife have the baby?"

"Let's play driving school. I'll steer, and you have a temper tantrum."

Perpetual emotion

The young newlywed sounded bewildered and desperate when he confided being unable to fulfill his connubial function. When I saw him again, I asked about the shot I'd given him to help overcome his difficulty. "At first, it worked great," he replied. "The first night was terrific. On Saturday and Sunday, everything still went fine in the morning and afternoon and night, and also Monday morning and lunchtime. But then, that evening, the same darn problem!"
— *John D. Rosen,* MD

"Come out, Mr. Wilkins. It's time for the meek to inherit the earth."

"I don't care *how* good she is at sniffing out drugs...."

"It sure beats that old 'Think' sign."

Cost-consciousness

I'd referred a patient with bleeding hemorrhoids to a proctologist, who was in the midst of inserting a sigmoidoscope when the patient asked: "Say, Doc, how much does that instrument cost?" The consultant inquired why he wanted to know. "Well," came the choked-up reply, "if it's going to hurt as much coming out as it did going in, I'll buy it and leave it there." — *Robert W. Begley,* MD

"You go in first and destroy his incentive."

"It wasn't worth getting cleaned up for."

"Please take your license out of your wallet, ma'am. I want to rip it into a million pieces."

Reply requested?

When my wife and I sat down to a late dinner, my head still felt clouded from all the dictating I'd one during a long and trying day—referral notes, other correspondence, histories, discharge summaries. I may have been more startled than she was as I was saying grace and found myself concluding with these words: "Thank you, Lord. End of dictation." — *Floyd F Miller,* MD

"So this is hell. Why, it looks just like my old office!"

"Somehow, it just doesn't seem like the first day of summer."

Snack time

During the wee hours, a beefy young man was brought into the emergency room with a gunshot wound just below his umbilicus. Hoping that his stomach would be empty because prompt surgery was obviously called for, I asked him when he last had anything to eat. "Don't worry about that, Doc,"he said. "I ain't very hungry." — *D.C. Coldsmith,* MD

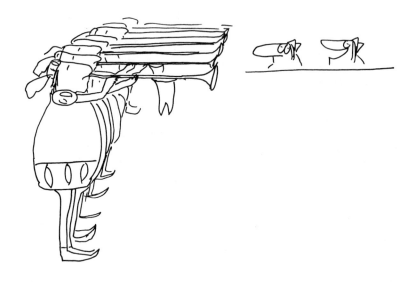

"I love this little flurry of excitement when the surgeon arrives."

"My computer says it's time for a cost-of-living adjust-
ment in my allowance."

"What the hell *does* make you happy?"

"Can we play with them, or do we have to wait and see which ones get recalled?"

"I'm glad I didn't opt for early retirement."

"It's very nice, Miss Willoughby, but take it down anyway."

"Let's face reality, Martha. DNA has programmed an unquenchable thirst into my genes."

Hardship case

A routine inquiry about non-payment of my office charges brought this reply from a patient: "Please send another copy of the bill, and I'll pay it after I get better and back to work if I can find a job and my wife and girlfriend have their babies and I get my truck fixed. That is, if I'm not in jail on the income tax charge."
— *Mary O. Anderson,* MD

"I'll remove the thorn if you'll sign this release."

"Apparently, it still has some bugs."

"I've yet to own a car that was user-friendly."

Rest now, pay later

"What's going on?" The question came from the young woman stretched out on a hard table following an exploratory laparotomy. "We're missing one sponge," the technician told her, "and we're taking an X-ray to look for it." "Never mind that," the patient mumbled drowsily. "Just add it to my bill and let me get back to sleep."   — *Russel W. Bagley,* MD

"For the last time, Fred—NO!"

"Oh, oh—Here comes trouble!"

"I'm sorry, but our chef seems to be having an off-day."

Change of address

My work at an extended care facility was disturbed by an elderly convalescent who constantly shrieked: "Nurse! Nurse! Nurse!" at the top of her lungs. After bearing up as long as I could, I went into the patient's room. I gently explained that all that screaming was annoying the nurses and resulting in her getting less, rather than more, attention. She said she understood and promised to stop doing it. Pleased by my tactful handling of the situation. I returned to my office. Just as I reached the desk, I heard a loud cry resounding down the hall: "Doctor! Doctor! Doctor!"   — *A. Pollack,* MD

"You say you jog ten miles a day. Is that to and from the refrigerator?"

"I want a perfume my husband will appreciate. Got anything that smells like a fishing trip?"

"I don't care *who* started it!"

Birds and bees

Called out in the night to a rundown house in a backwoods area, I was greeted by a woman who brought me into a bedroom where her 16-year-old grand-daughter was writhing in labor. After delivering a healthy 8-pound girl, I sat down to fill out the birth record. When I came to the line calling for the name of the baby's father, I asked who he was. "Doc," the grandmother answered, "that's like putting your hand in a beehive and trying to figure out which one stung you."
— *A.P. Warthman,* DO

"Yeah, I watch the channel with the funny weatherman, too."

"It's nothing to worry about. Listen—I had the same thing, only worse."

"Double scotch—and hurry!"

Cutting compliment

One of my former associates received a letter marked "personal" some months after he performed a double aortocoronary bypass on a 54-year-old man with severe angina. The letter came from the patient's wife as an unsolicited testimonial to the doctor's surgical skill. "You done such a good job on that old buzzard," it read, "that he run off with a 24-year-old hussy. Wish now you had cut his throat.   — *R.M. Shepard,* MD

"Imagine how much it would be if I had to carry malpractice insurance."

"Well, I don't know...five hundred dollars is a lot for *any* parrot."

"What's this I hear about your metabolism slowing down?"

Less cause for worry

After the myelogram done on an internist friend of mine showed a ruptured disk, the neurosurgeon told him he'd have to wait a few days for the laminectomy to be performed. The patient asked why. "Our anesthesiologist is out of town," was the answer. "You can get one of the nurse anesthetists to work with you," the internists suggested. "Oh, no," the surgeon replied. "This is a tricky operation, and your hypertension and diabetes are additional complications. If one of the nurses put you to sleep and something happened to you, she'd never get over it. The anesthesiologist would get over it."

— *Swan Burrus Jr.,* MD

"I'll need to see your driver's license and two major credit cards."

"I know we need the money, but no wife of mine is going to work!"

"Perhaps you'd prefer to come back some other time, sir?"

Such is fame

One of my neighboring colleagues received a midnight phone call asking him to make an emergency visit to the opposite end of town. "Father's just died," the caller explained, "and we need someone to sign the death certificate." The doctor suggested that the family should get in touch with some other physician closer by. "Oh, no," was the reply. "We want you. You've been very highly recommended."   — *Herbert Mallison,* MD

"Great birthday party...three squad cars!"

"I'm going to tell you what your stocks did yesterday.
Take some deep breaths."

"...then left, then right, then two lefts, then right, then left, then three rights, then...."

Quick learner

I was doing a preschool examination on a bright and inquisitive youngster, who informed me he wanted to be a doctor when he grew up. After he asked me to explain how "the blood pressure thing" worked, he nodded and said, "That's neat." Smiling, I remarked, "Now you can hang out your shingle." A puzzled look came over his face. Then it disappeared, and he hopped off the table and began to unzip.   — *G.H. Berndsen,* MD

"Anything important on the news tonight? Like your forgetting my birthday?"

"After careful deliberation, Your Honor, we'd rather not get involved."

"You've taken this bureaucratic mumbo-jumbo and turned it into language that people in all stations of life can understand. Curtis, you're fired!"

Blues in the night

Awakened by the phone at 3 a.m., I was puzzled when the patient said: "Doc, those pills I took are killing me." Not having seen him for some time, I asked what pills he meant and when I'd prescribed them. "Oh, I didn't get them from you," he said. "I had an earache this morning and at lunch time I went to Dr. Miller in my building." Wide awake now, I asked, "Why don't you call *him*?" He answered in a tone of mingled surprise and annoyance: "Call *him*? But *you're* my doctor."

— *S. Isenberg,* DO

"It's done wonders for Pamela. She puts her roller skates away now without my saying a word."

"Edith, why didn't you tell me Jimmy's home from college for the weekend?"

That's the ticket

One of the physicians at our rural hospital was known to use his busy schedule as an excuse for whizzing along the roads with little regard for the speed limit. One morning, when he was leaving to make his rounds, he gave in to his 5-year-old son's urging to take him along for the ride. When they returned home, his wife asked the little boy if he'd enjoyed the trip. "It was swell," he replied. "especially when a nice man on a motorcycle stopped us and wrote Daddy a prescription."
                                                                    — *Lee H. Vensel,* MD

"What the hell, try it. You're only ninety once."

"I *am* married—but I want a second opinion."

Stop, look, and listen

Fatigue after a long day in the office helped show me early in my practice how important it is to let patients ventilate their anxieties. I was alone and ready to close shop when an elderly lady came in. She sat down and immediately launched a recital of her symptoms. As her monologue rattled on non-stop for more than 15 minutes, I was too tired to produce anything but an occasional "Yes" or "Uh-huh." Then she sprang up, offered a handshake, and said: "I'm so glad I came. You're the first doctor who has ever understood my problems."

— *Earl J. Levine,* MD

"Wasn't it sweet of him to take me by the station to pick you up?"

"Bad enough she got the house, the car, and the kids. The judge even gave her custody of my starting time."

"It has a cold, it wants chicken soup, and we can all go to blazes!"

Petty disturbance

One night recently, I received an urgent call at home from the mother of a patient of another pediatrician for whom I was covering. "My daughter came home from school today with head lice," she told me. "I used the Kwell shampoo on her, my husband, and myself. Should I also use it on our cat?" I tried to keep cool as I replied: "Why don't you call your veterinarian?" Her voice registered shock as she said, "What? At this hour?" — *Joseph F. J. Curi,* MD

"Look at it philosophically. Doesn't this make all your other troubles seem insignificant?"

"It *is* a lot to pay for such a short visit. Tell you what, next time I'll leave the sigmoidoscope in for ten minutes longer."

"Go ahead, but don't say I didn't warn you."

A rash decision

A severe leg rash prompted a man from a rural area to come to town to be examined by one of my colleagues. After history-taking and a series of tests, the physician advised the patient that he'd better get rid of the dog that was evidently causing an allergic reaction. Mainly out of curiosity, my friend asked the man as he rose to go if he planned to sell the animal or give it away. "Neither one," the patient replied. "I'm going to get me one of them second opinions I been reading about. It's a lot easier to find a doctor than a good bird dog." — *George Hawkins,* MD

"If I hum the National Anthem, will you sign off?"

"*Please* come out, Mr. Downey. The doctor was just trimming the hedge while he waited for you to get here for your vasectomy."

Rear opening

While at my desk one Saturday to catch up on paperwork, I picked up the phone to hear a woman ask: "How long will you be open?" Not thinking to ask if she had the right number, I said: "The office is closed, but can I help you?" Since I specialize in rectal problems, I'll never forget the mental picture conjured up by her next question: "Do you have a drive-in window?"

— *E. Aubrey Cox,* MD

"Binson, your reputation has already gone down the drain. Would you do something distasteful for me?"

"Have you ever considered hovering over a stadium?"

"What they want is for me to make them feel good enough to go back to doing the things that make them feel bad."

Blind spot

After a power failure gave me a scare while I was finishing a minor surgical procedure, a colleague told me about an experience he'd had during a previous blackout. The internist had been in a windowless room performing a cystoscopy. Just as he was probing the prostate, the room turned pitch black. "What did you do to me, Doc?" the patient screamed. "I can't see a thing!"

— *Carl E. Kierney,* MD

AUTOS

"That's $7,897.99 for the car, plus tax. Now, would you like it assembled?"

"Would you do me a favor and put on your bikini? I'm trying to get Lou to mow the lawn."

"Our sermon this morning will be brief."

In a brown wrapping?

Not long before her third child was due, a young mother came in with her small son and daughter. I smilingly asked them what they were hoping Mommy would have. The boy answered for both of them: "Suzy wants a sister, and I want a brother. So we been wondering if you couldn't just make it a plain baby."

— *Edwin T. MacCamy,* MD

"I don't know how he manages it. Most of us just hit our thumbs."

"Read the invitation again. I invited your *dog*—not you."

"It's hard to understand how TV can be a wasteland
when they use so much fertilizer."

Why do you ask?

Blood work was indicated when my 3-year-old son developed ankle pains that resisted diagnosis. With no other physician available in my hospital's lab at the time, I undertook to draw blood but failed to extract a drop after two attempts. A technician took over and succeeded on the first try. My son was waiting at the door when I came home that evening. "Daddy," he asked, "are you really a doctor?"
— *Robert H. Leonard., MD*

"Why don't you stick with that dog food while you're ahead?"

"Gee, I don't know what to do when someone faints, either. We never learned first aid—just sex education."

"The mechanic looked me straight in the eye, gave a
nasty laugh, and said, 'Learn to live with it, Doc'."

"The string? Oh, yeah—I love you."

"Been here long?"

"It's our tax forms!"

True confession?

As my wife and I were leaving the house to make a condolence visit, our 5-year-old daughter asked where we were going. "Mrs. Green's father died," I answered, "and we want to tell her we're sorry." She gave me a piercing look and then asked: "Why? Did you do it?" — *Howard H. Bearman*, MD

"That's Latin for 'tough luck'."

"Who you callin' a momma's boy?!"

"That should be healed by the time I finish filling out this insurance claim."

It's all relative

"How good is he?" the elderly lady asked when I suggested a consultant for what seemed to be surgical problem. "Excellent," I said. "I even had him operate on my mother." She was silent for a long moment, then she gave me a piercing look as she asked: "Doctor, do you love your mother?"

— *Cyrill S. C. Moore,* MD

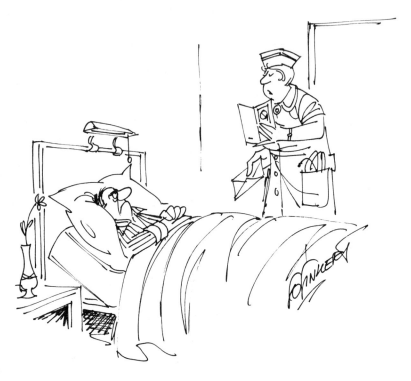

"It's a sympathy card from your office staff to the nurses."

"Stop this foolishness and tell him I'm not for sale!"

Optimal outcome

I told the waiting mother that her 16-year-old son's surgery had gone very well. "That must be a big relief for you" was her surprising reply. "For me?" I asked. "Of course," she said. "My son asked me last night if I was going to sue you if everything didn't turn out all right." — *Joseph S. Neigut,* MD

"All right, I'll play house with you. But don't expect me to
give up my career."

"Dudley is a man of many parts—none of which has ever worked."

"I don't know, Tonto....Pension plans can be awfully ex-
pensive."

"However, *my* trained corporate eye sees something entirely different."

"I'm afraid I don't have any cash on me. Do you have a toll-free number I could call?"

"May we have a moment of silence, please? After an extended illness, our beloved checkbook passed away today."

All you need to know

It took some time to persuade our part-time maid to write down all the details whenever she took phone messages while we were out. Finally, I found this note taped to the phone: "Man's voice . Didn't say name. Said you a dam dope and hung up."   — *Levon D. Yazujian,* MD

"Pop, can I have the pieces after you tear it up...like last time?"

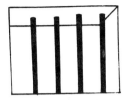

"The usual story—I started out opening childproof bottle caps. After that, bank vaults were easy."

"I can't be the world's worst wife. That would be too much of a coincidence."

"If you didn't plan on buying me a dog, why did you have
me in the first place?"

"This is my fiftieth holdup, and I wanted it to be memorable."

"Mind making a dash for it, Mr. Grogan? It breaks up the office routine."

Bump and run

As acting coroner, I came to the hospital late one night to check on the victim of a fatal accident. An orderly accompanied me down the dimly lit hall in the basement that led to the morgue. Aware that the pathologist sometimes worked behind a locked door, I knocked three times. At that, the orderly piped up: "If anyone answers, I'm leaving."   — *Francis N. Taylor,* MD

"Can we grant people asylum from the IRS?"

"That's disgusting, Thelma!"

"I hope this is for real. One week in a foster home, and I always wind up back here."

"Remember one thing, Herbert—You've got a pacemaker in you, not a miracle maker."

"You're the dermatologist. *You* adjust the flesh tones."

"I'd be willing to pay a little extra for a line of credit."

"It has something to do with my dad just looking cross-eyed at her."

For mercy's sake!

The kindergarten teacher was asking the new pupils what kind of work their fathers did. When my son's turn came, he said I was a psychiatrist. She asked him to tell the class what a psychiatrist does. Without a moment's hesitation, he explained: "When someone tries to kill themselves, he helps them."

— *Donald R. Grayson,* MD

"I did have a house in the price range you mention. I sold it back in 1975."

"It's not so bad. At least he visits now and then to play with the kids."

"Your chest cleared? Good—I'll prescribe the same
medicine for your check."

Hell's bells

Early in my career, as I went into the recovery room to see a patient coming out of anesthesia, far-off church chimes sounded. "I must be in heaven," the patient murmured dreamily. Then she saw me. "No, I can't be," she said. "There's Dr. Campbell."   — *Lenore D. Campbell,* MD

"I hate it when he does that."

"Your Honor, my client is prepared to plead guilty to the lesser charge of double-parking in front of the bank while the holdup was in progress."

"Could you help us? We seem to have lost the Meadow-lark Country Club."

Severest critic

When my grandson was 4 years old, he banged his hand while playing. Seeing that the bruise wasn't serious. I gently kissed his hand and said, "Now it will be all better." As he walked away, I heard him mutter: "Boy! What dumb doctor!"
— *George S. Gordon,* MD

"I've always admired your frankness, George."

"About the instructions you put on Mr. Grouchley's sup-
positories...."

"It's just a thought, gentlemen, but the employees
might be easier to handle if we reorganized as a cult."

"I don't want you to see who's coming tomorrow. You need a good night's sleep."

"Honey, I think I liked you better before you took up aerobics."

"If you ask me, there are a lot of things we need worse."

"Ralph, can you hear me? If a woman from Accounting comes by and says she's a witch, *don't laugh!*"

"It was my legal savvy that won the case. That's why I'm entitled to eighty percent of the settlement. Any idiot can get knocked down by a bus."

"Please, Melanie...I can *change*."

"Some people are party animals. Millard is a party vege-
table."

"How soon can I tell her about her prized crystal bowl?"

"Looks like they're forceably retiring Figley."

"Can I borrow one of your suits, Dad? Tomorrow is 'Nerd Day' at school."

"A lot of good it did me to send you to obedience school!"

Competitive bidding

"I'll give you a dime if you let me look down your throat," I said cajolingly to the balky 8-year-old patient. "I'll give you a quarter," she retorted, "if you'll leave me alone."

— Syed A. Hoda, MD

"It's my patriotic duty to ask for a raise. If I get one, the country will benefit from the added taxes I'll pay."

"Actually, my dear, I did not forget. I've been sitting here all evening offering silent toasts to our wedding anniversary."

"Dietrich, is this job too much for you?"

"It's seventy-five dollars extra if you want to sit next to a sky marshal."

"The operation was a complete success, except that I've lost my contact lenses somewhere."

"Never say 'I dare you!' to a judge."

"I'm wondering about the acoustics. Yell at me, Agnes."

Cash on the line

The young woman was four months pregnant. She came in for a routine visit, accompanied by her 4-year-old son. "Can we take the baby home with us now?" he asked. "Not yet," I answered with a smile. He persisted: "If Mommy pays for him now, can we have him?"
— *J. Michael Epps,* MD

"Just how naughty do I have to be before I blow it?"

"And the following response to that lunatic editorial is
made under a grant from me—J. Elwood Griggs!"

"I'd replace him with a computer, but they don't make any that simple."

"Why should I believe you about the birds and bees? You lied about the tooth fairy."

"I think there's a better solution to this."

"And for exercise, I want you to talk a long walk every day—while everybody else is eating dinner."

"Yes, we have electric typewriters."

Dead to the world

To reassure the tearful little boy on the cart, I said: "You'll be able to go home very soon, after I take your tonsils out." Looking at me, he wailed, "You aren't going to do it while I'm still alive, are you?" — *N.V. Lincoln,* MD

"I'm afraid there's only one thing to do—give him tennis lessons."

"Light your corncob pipe."

Unripe old age

I told the patient he could wait a year before returning for another eye exam. "I sure hope I'll be around," he replied. "I'm 78 years old, and I don't even buy green bananas any more."   — *Franklin A. Crystal,* MD

"We have a relatively simple incentive system here."

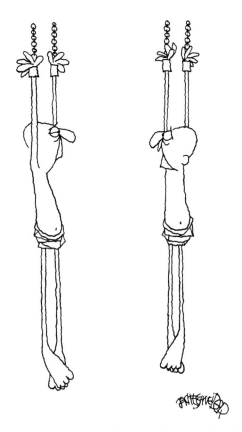

"What a coincidence! I was a No man, too."

"When Doctor Goldberg writes an order, he means business!"

Attendant illness

The dress code in our state's mental hospital was changed, allowing members of the staff to wear ordinary street clothing. "How can you tell them from the patients?" the superintendent was asked. "The patients get better," he said.

— *Frank Gable,* MD

"I told you it would work."

"I was negotiating with a congressman for his soul. Then somehow, I wound up giving him a campaign contribution."

"Henry started jogging today. He looks more youthful and athletic already."

Darned upstart

"He's older than he looks," I reassured the elderly lady, who seemed to have reservations about the young physician taking over my practice. "He's 32 years old," I explained. "Huh!" she snorted. "I've got socks older than that."

— J.B. Warren, MD

Can you believe it—they've *all* got headaches!"

"I'm afraid your sense of taste will never return. Your taste buds are completely worn out."

"I couldn't get the front end aligned, so I drove in reverse all day."

Played for a sucker

After examining him, I handed a 4-year-old patient a lollipop. "What do you say, dear?" his mother prompted. Frowning, he turned to me and said: "I thought you gave toys."   — *Leo R. Westmoreland Jr.,* MD

"Well, from here on, try to have a nice day."

"No Christmas bonus on my allowance?"

"He says he spent it all, and that he only wishes he could have been there for the reading of the will."

"Now, isn't that interesting! That's exactly the same second opinion I got from Doctor Roscoe, Doctor Glass, Doctor Watts, and...."

"I give up. Where's the patient?"